Zuzanna Kwiecien

An Odyssey of Wonder

(A Bewitching Colouring Book of Nature and Imagination)

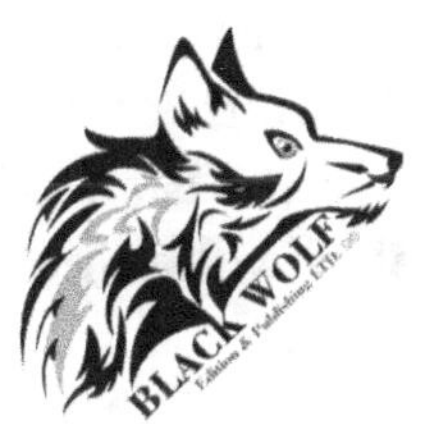

ISBN : 978-0-9934922-4-2
SKU/ID: ZK-01-16-ACB-0002

Copyrighted Work by Patamu.com
Registered Year 2016

Cover and illustrations by: Zuzanna Kwiecien
Preface by: Monica Turoni
Layout by: Black Wolf Edition & Publishing Ltd.

Publishing Company:
Black Wolf Edition & Publishing Ltd.
39 East Leven Street Burntisland KY3 9DX, Scotland
www.blackwolfedition.com

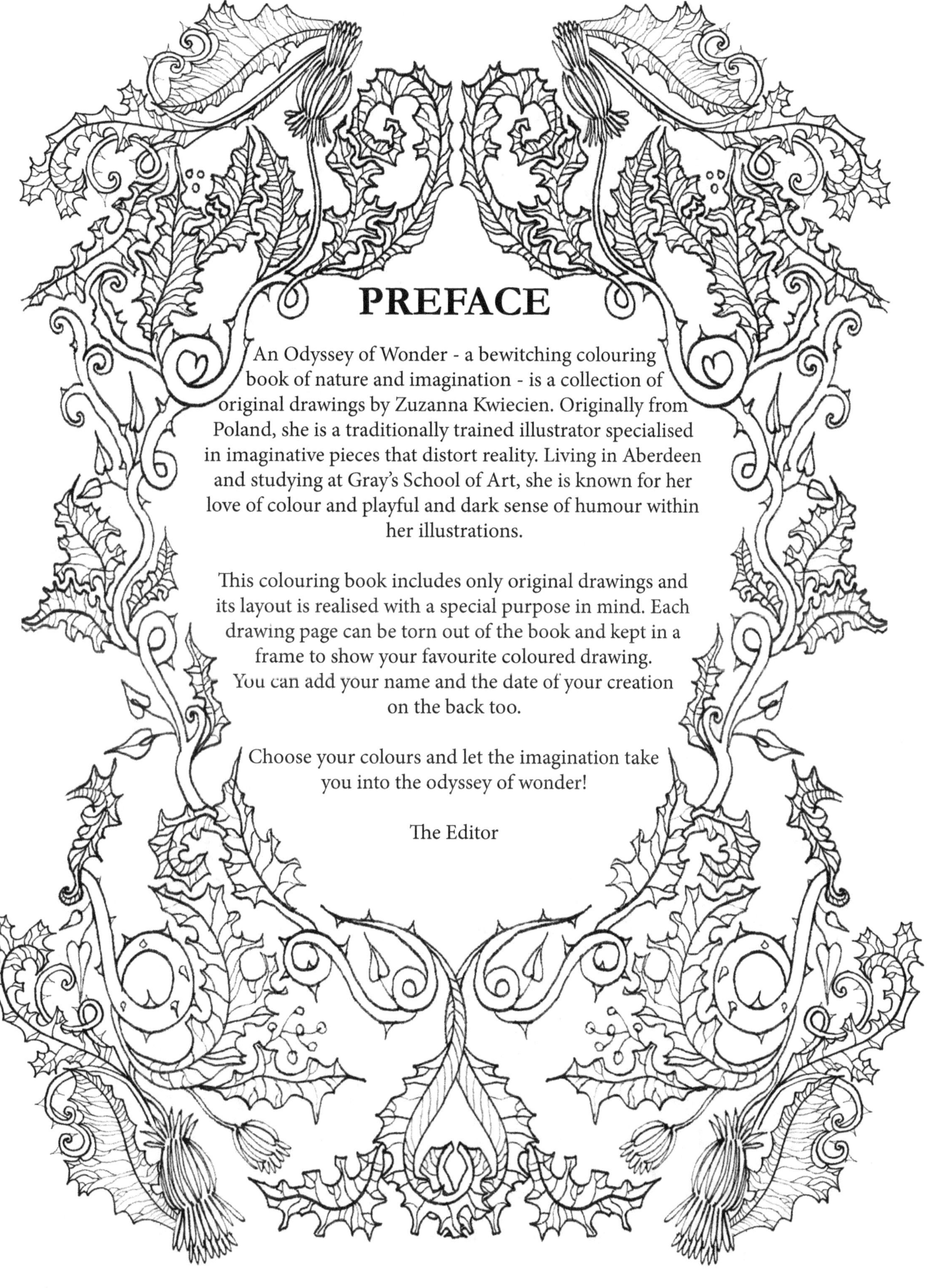

PREFACE

An Odyssey of Wonder - a bewitching colouring book of nature and imagination - is a collection of original drawings by Zuzanna Kwiecien. Originally from Poland, she is a traditionally trained illustrator specialised in imaginative pieces that distort reality. Living in Aberdeen and studying at Gray's School of Art, she is known for her love of colour and playful and dark sense of humour within her illustrations.

This colouring book includes only original drawings and its layout is realised with a special purpose in mind. Each drawing page can be torn out of the book and kept in a frame to show your favourite coloured drawing. You can add your name and the date of your creation on the back too.

Choose your colours and let the imagination take you into the odyssey of wonder!

The Editor

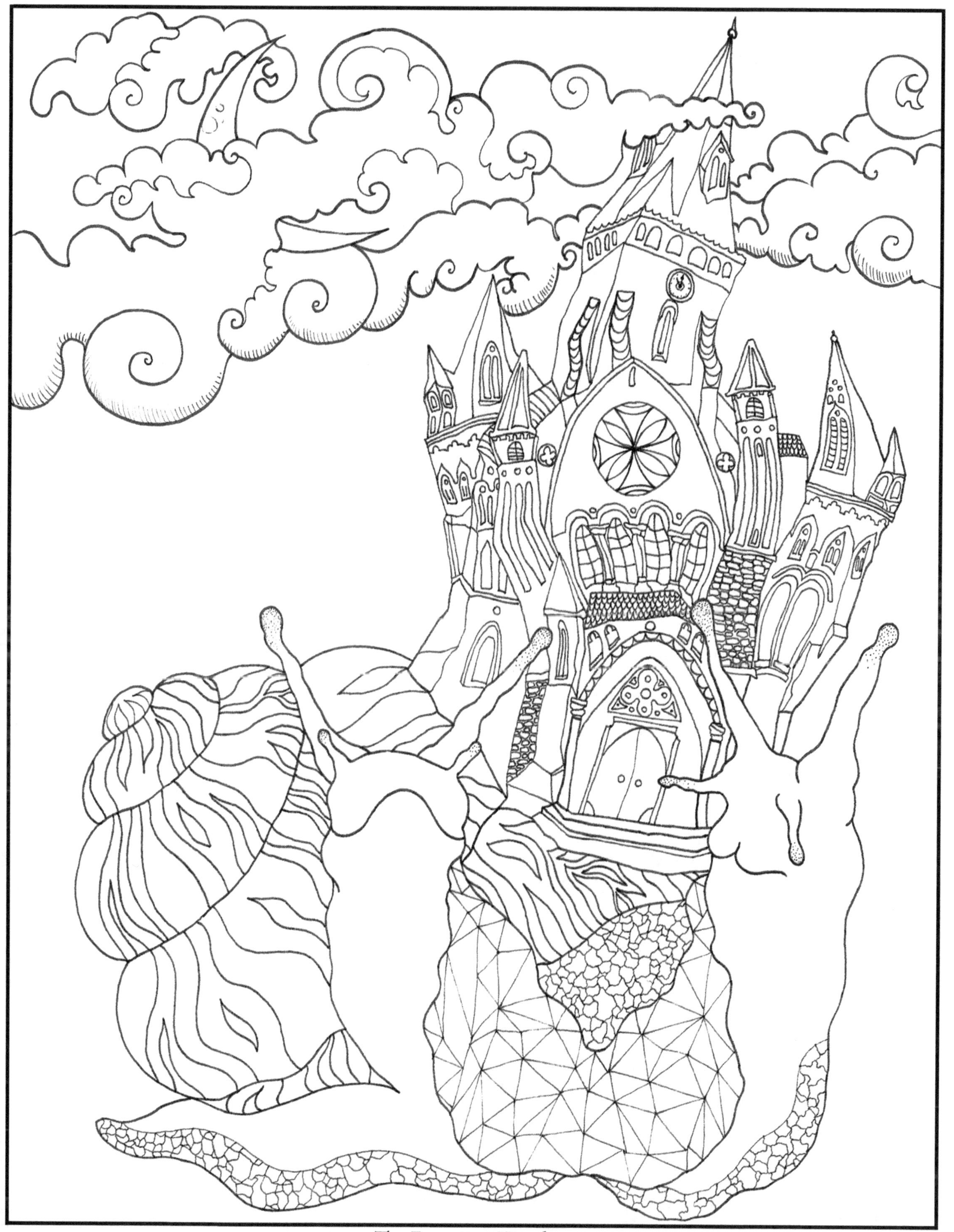

The Forgotten Kingdom

Coloured By:

....

Date: ....

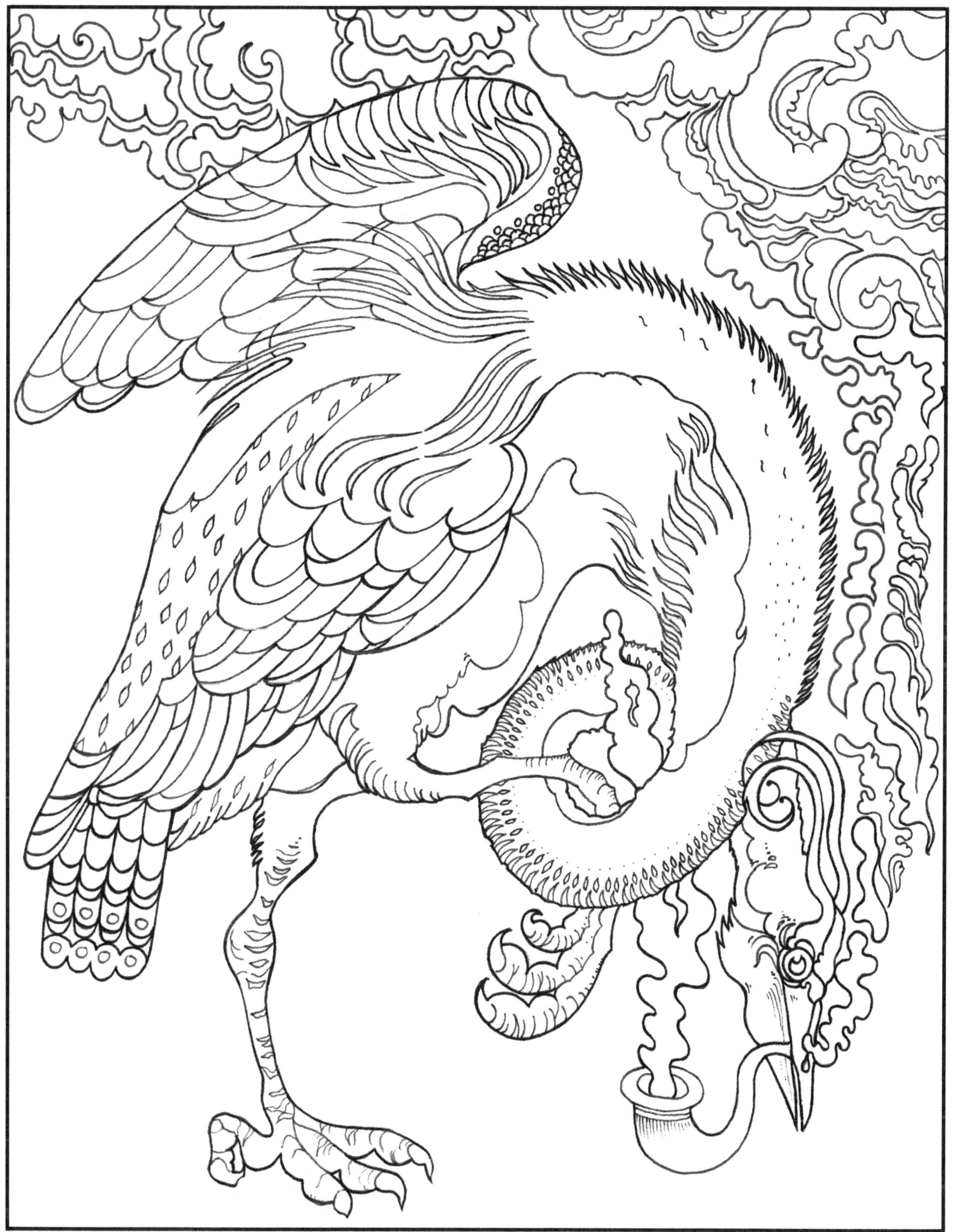

Why do Clouds Float

Coloured By:

....

Date: ....

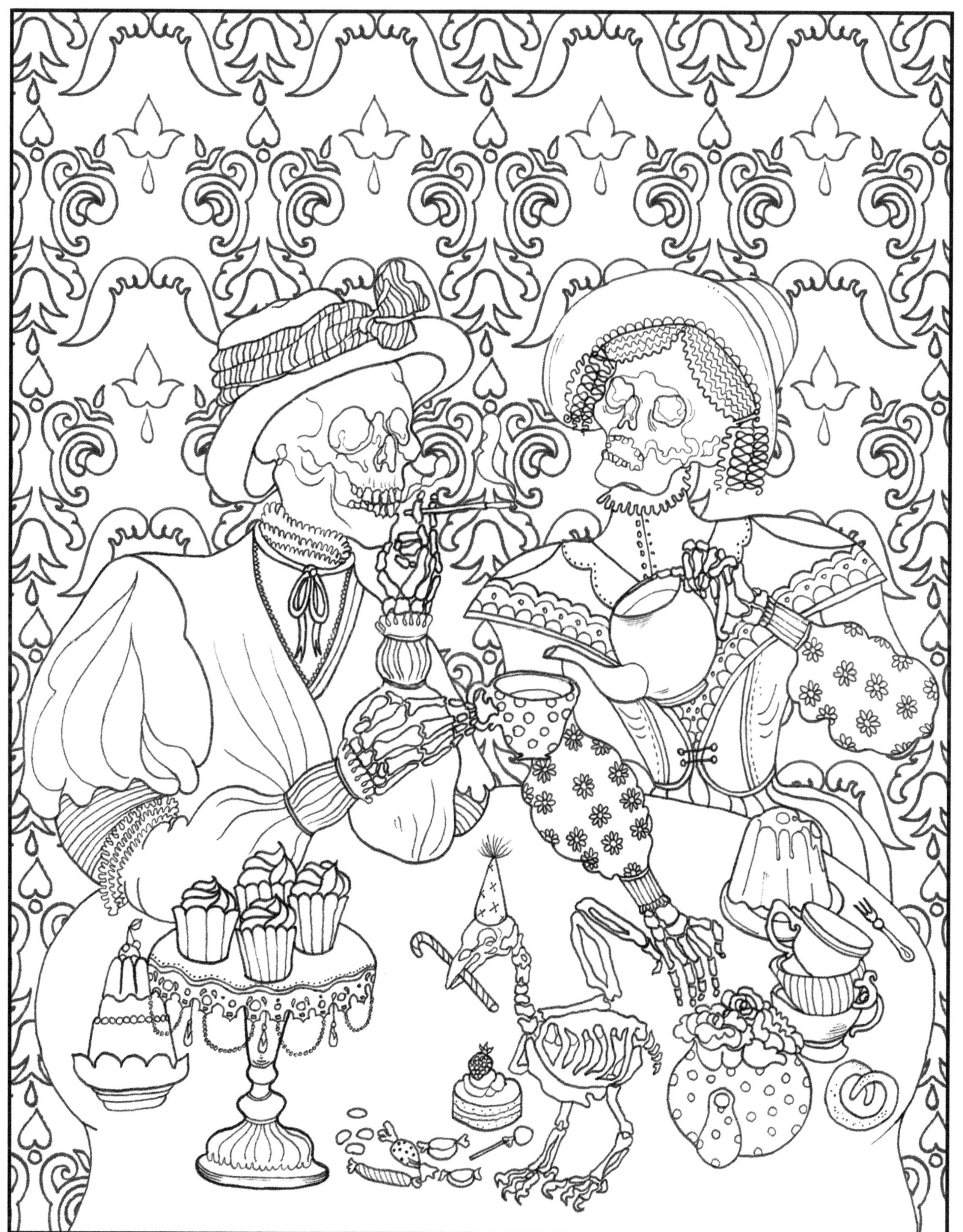

The Lurking Death of a Tea Party

Coloured By:

....

Date: ....

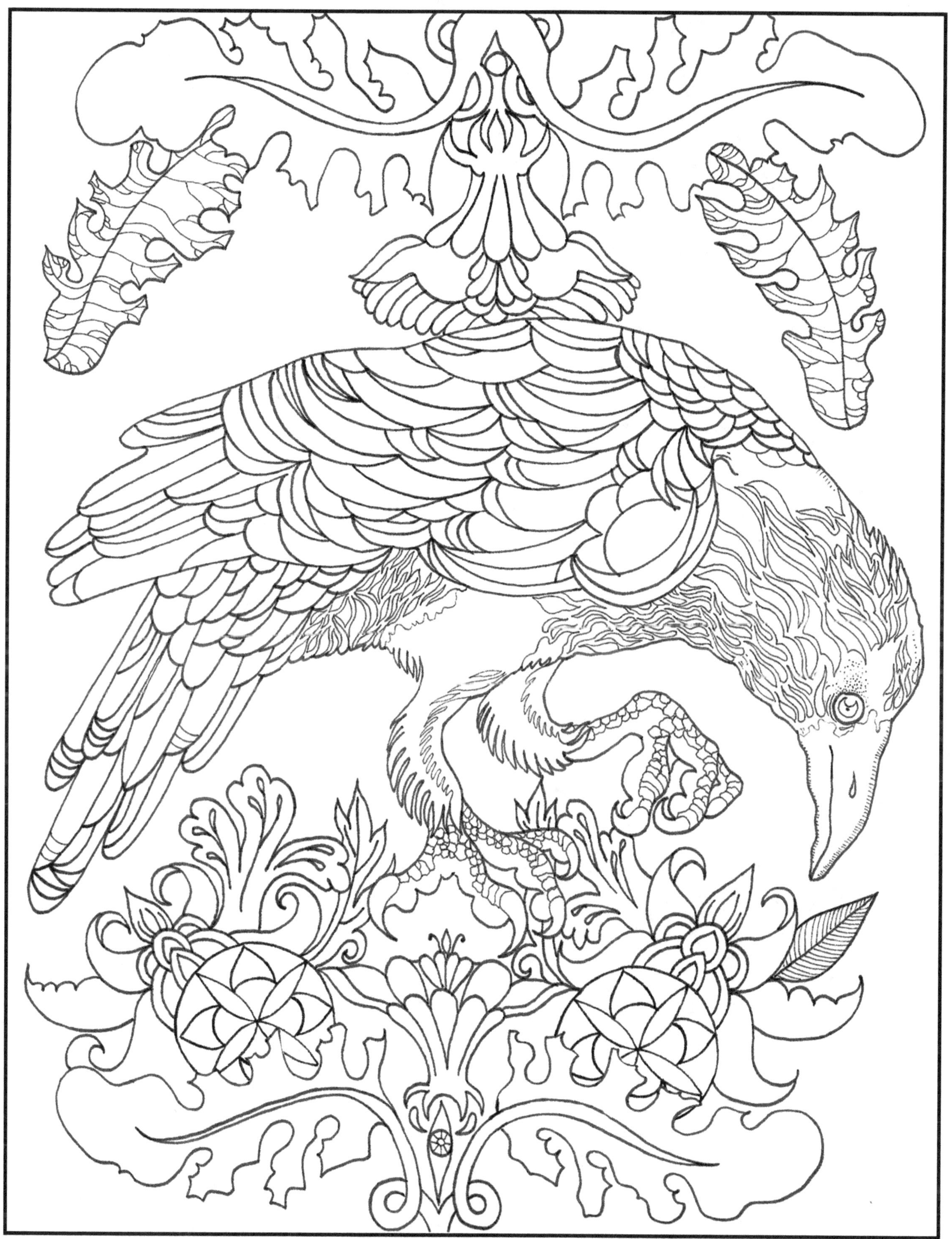

Ethan's Favourite Dream

Coloured By:

....

Date: ....

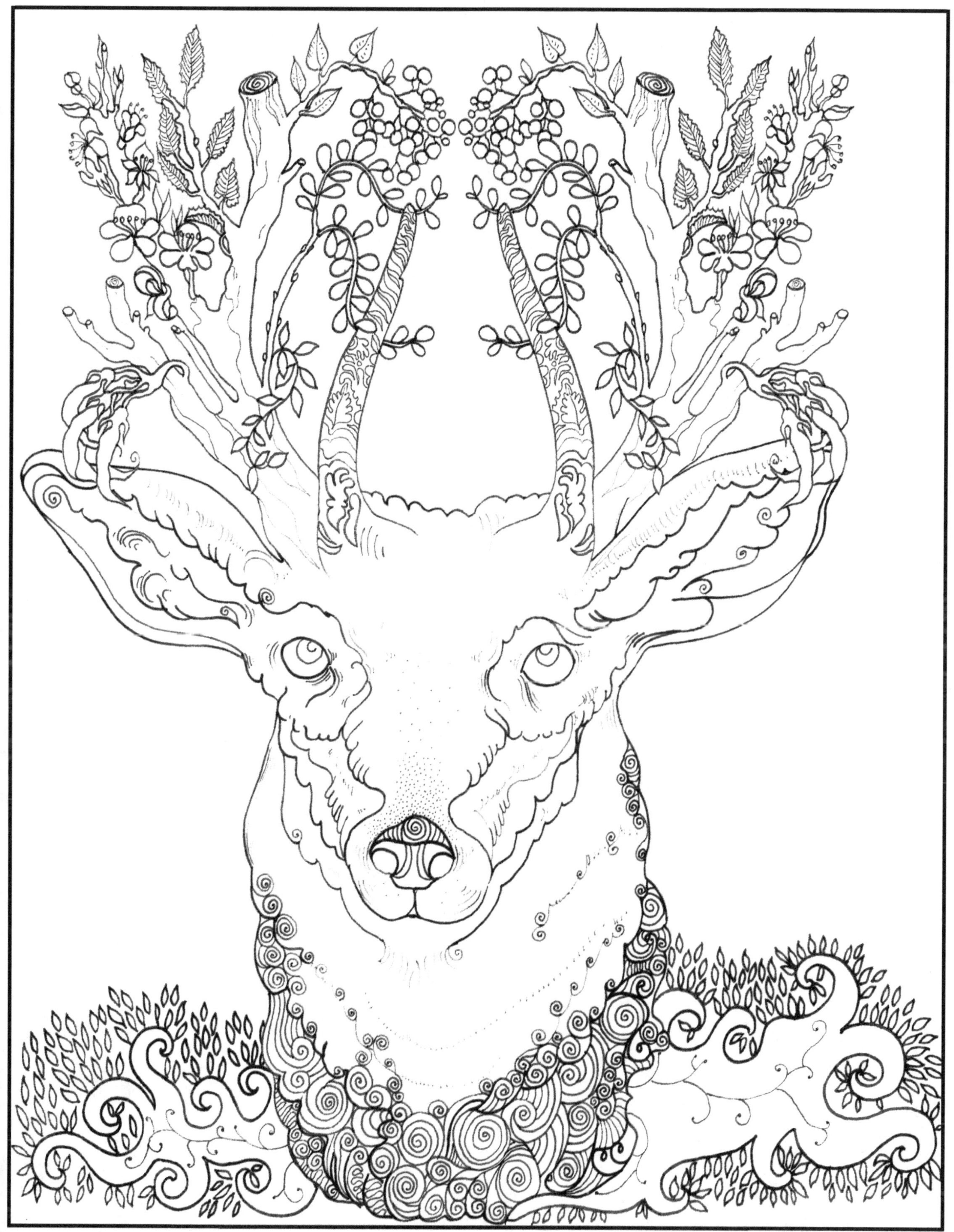

Springtime Spirit

Coloured By:

....

Date: ....

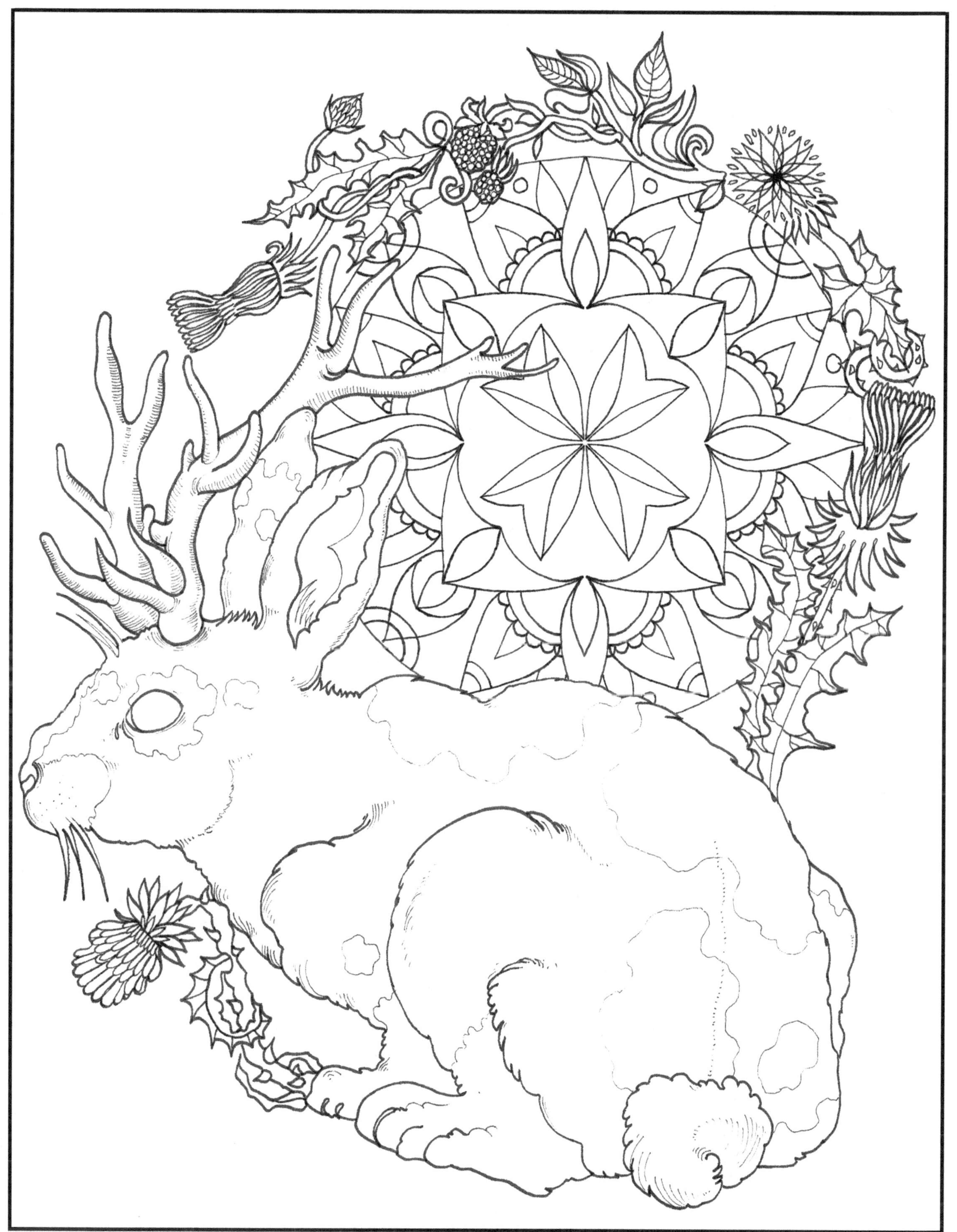

Rumoured to be Extinct

Coloured By:

....

Date: ....

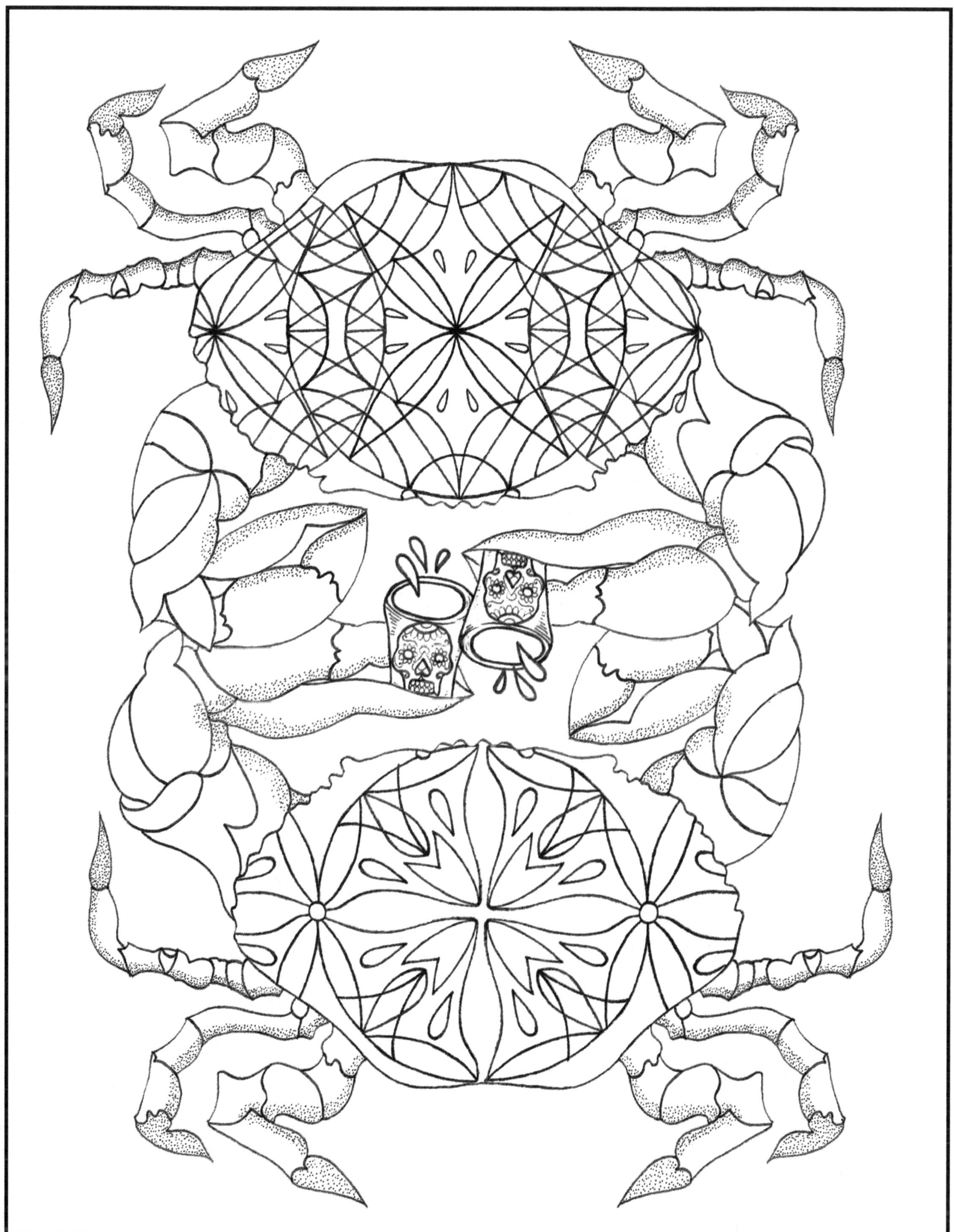

Soul Mates

Coloured By:

....

Date: ....

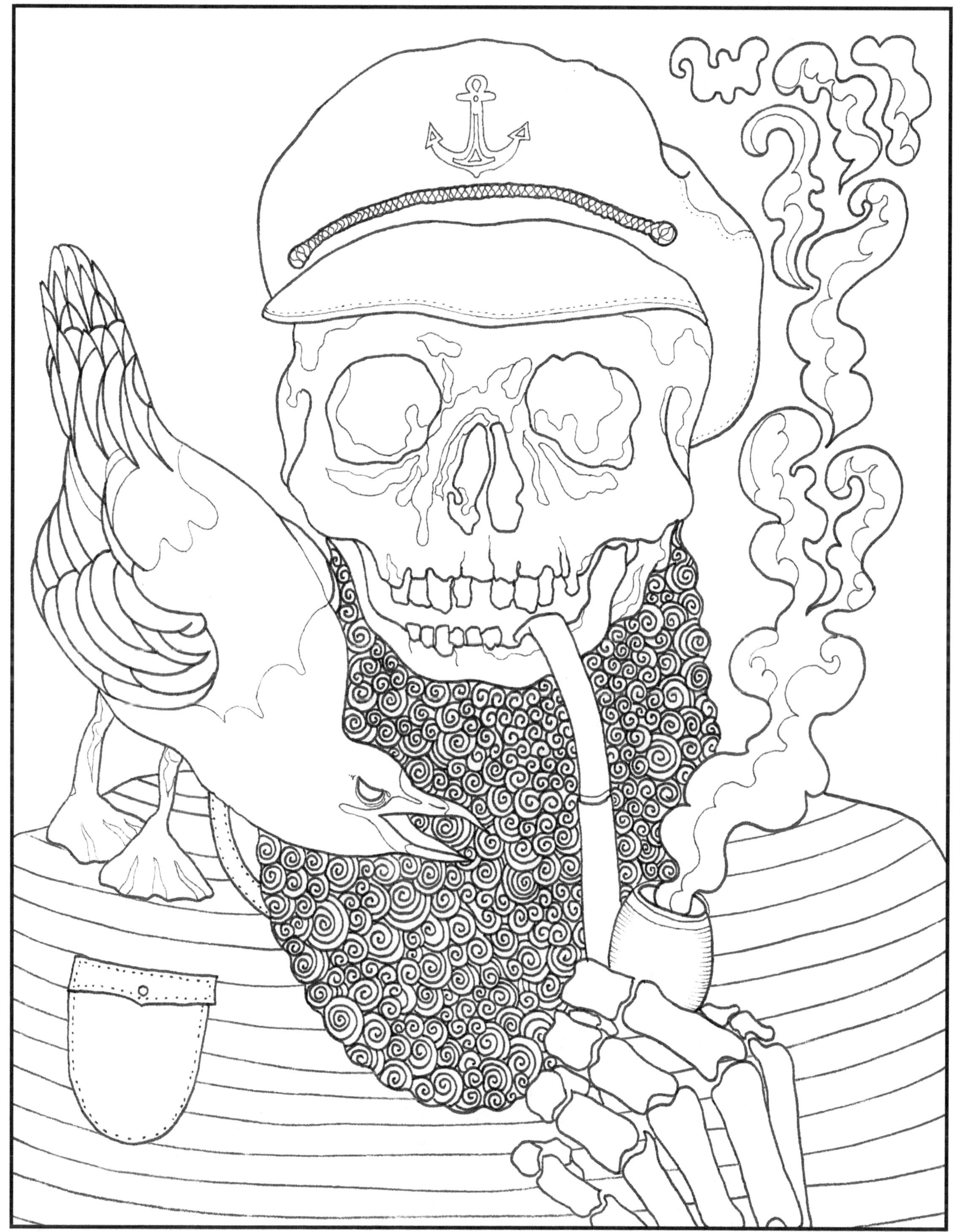

Welcome to Aberdeen

Coloured By:

....

Date: ....

Coloured By:

....

Date: ....

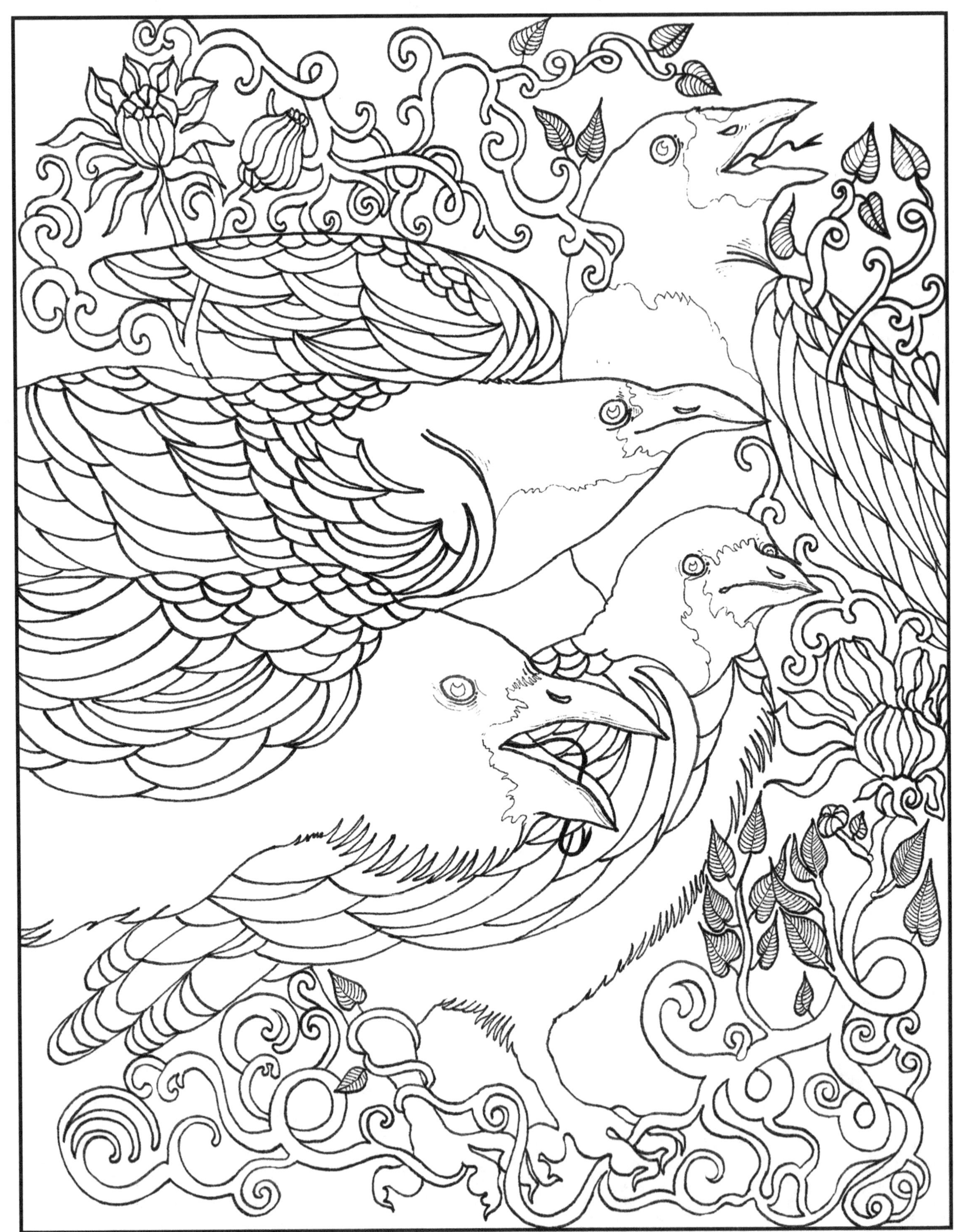

At Nightfall

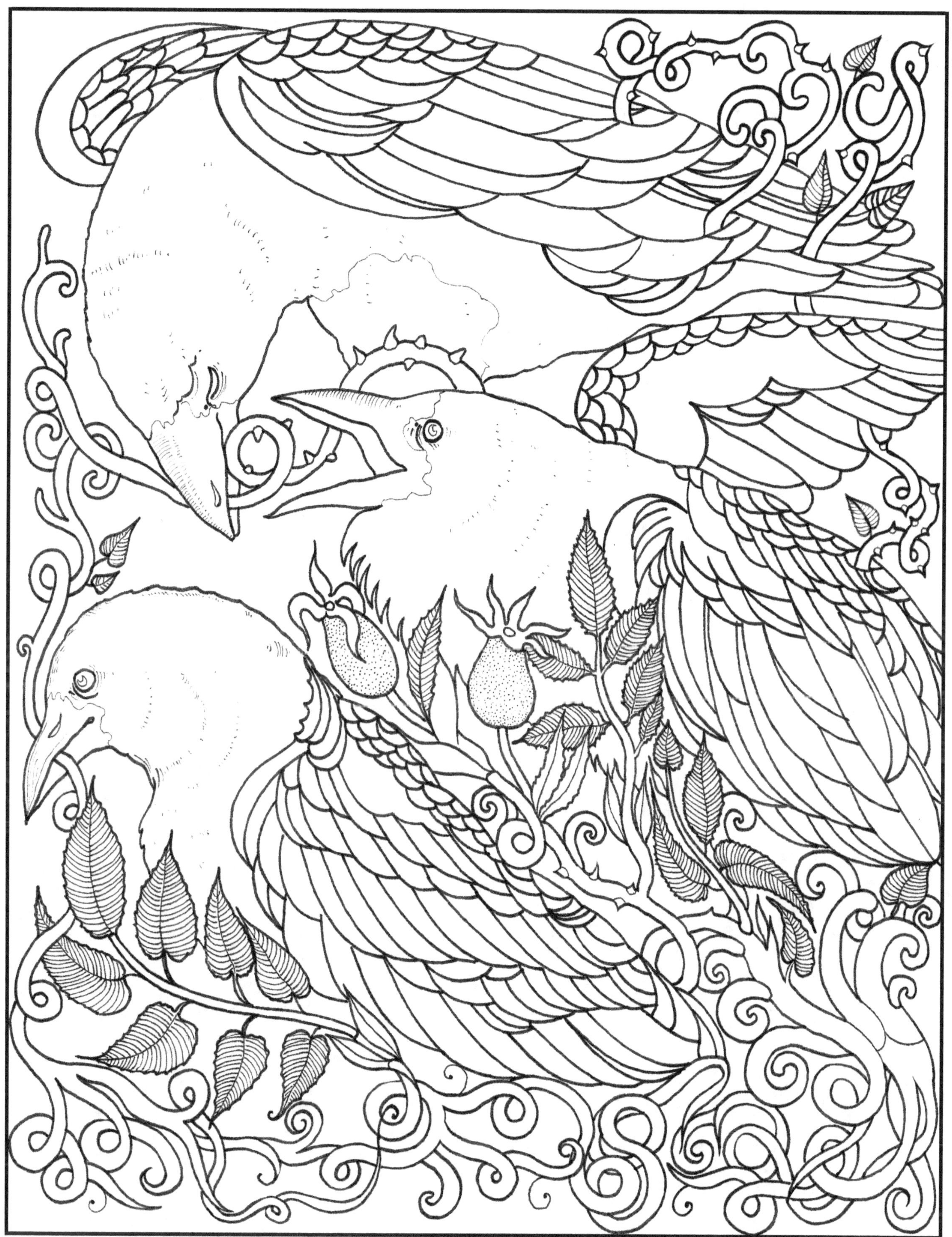

At Nightfall

Coloured By:

....

Date: ....

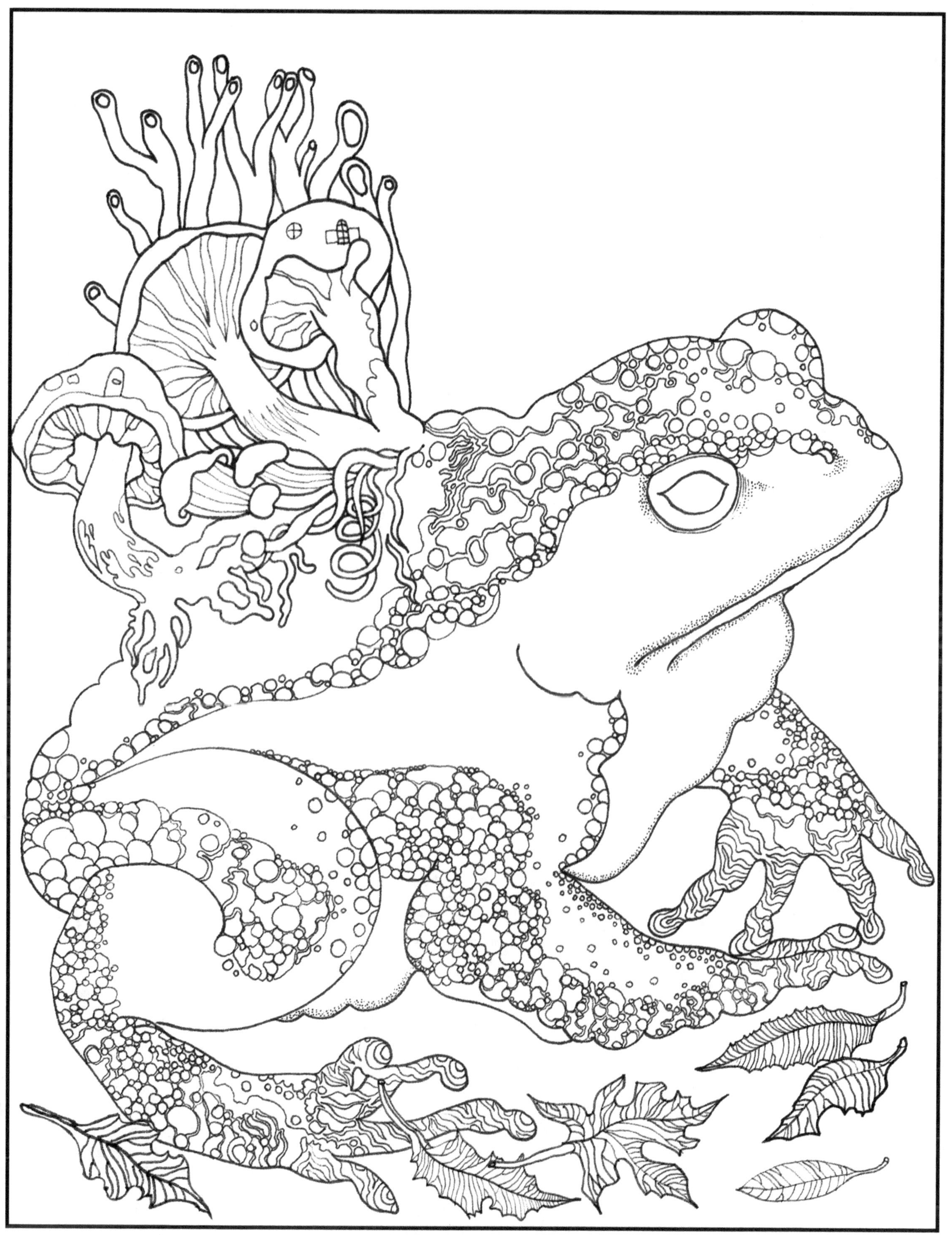

Once upon an Autumn Day

Coloured By:

....

Date: ....

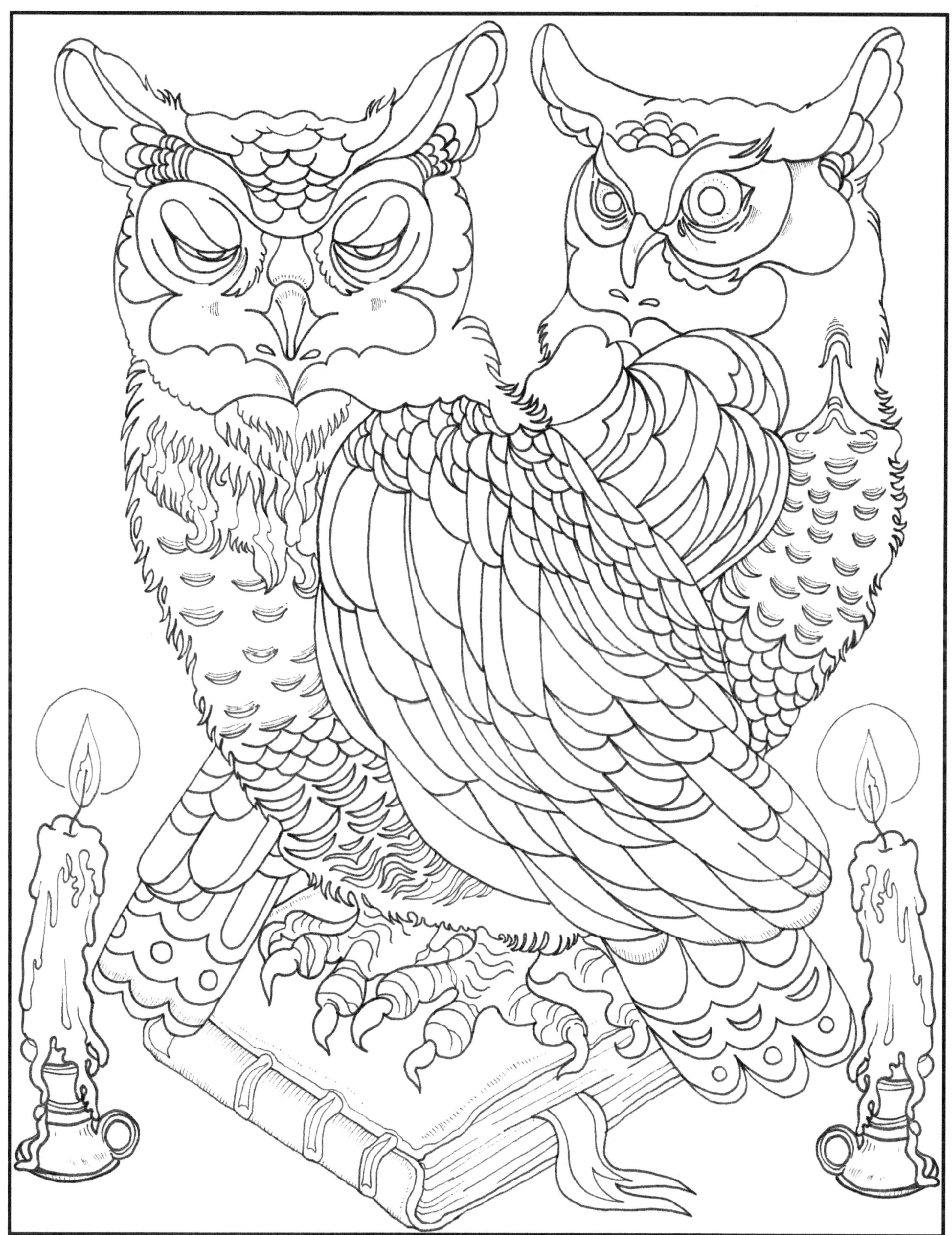

Keep Quiet

Coloured By:

....

Date: ....

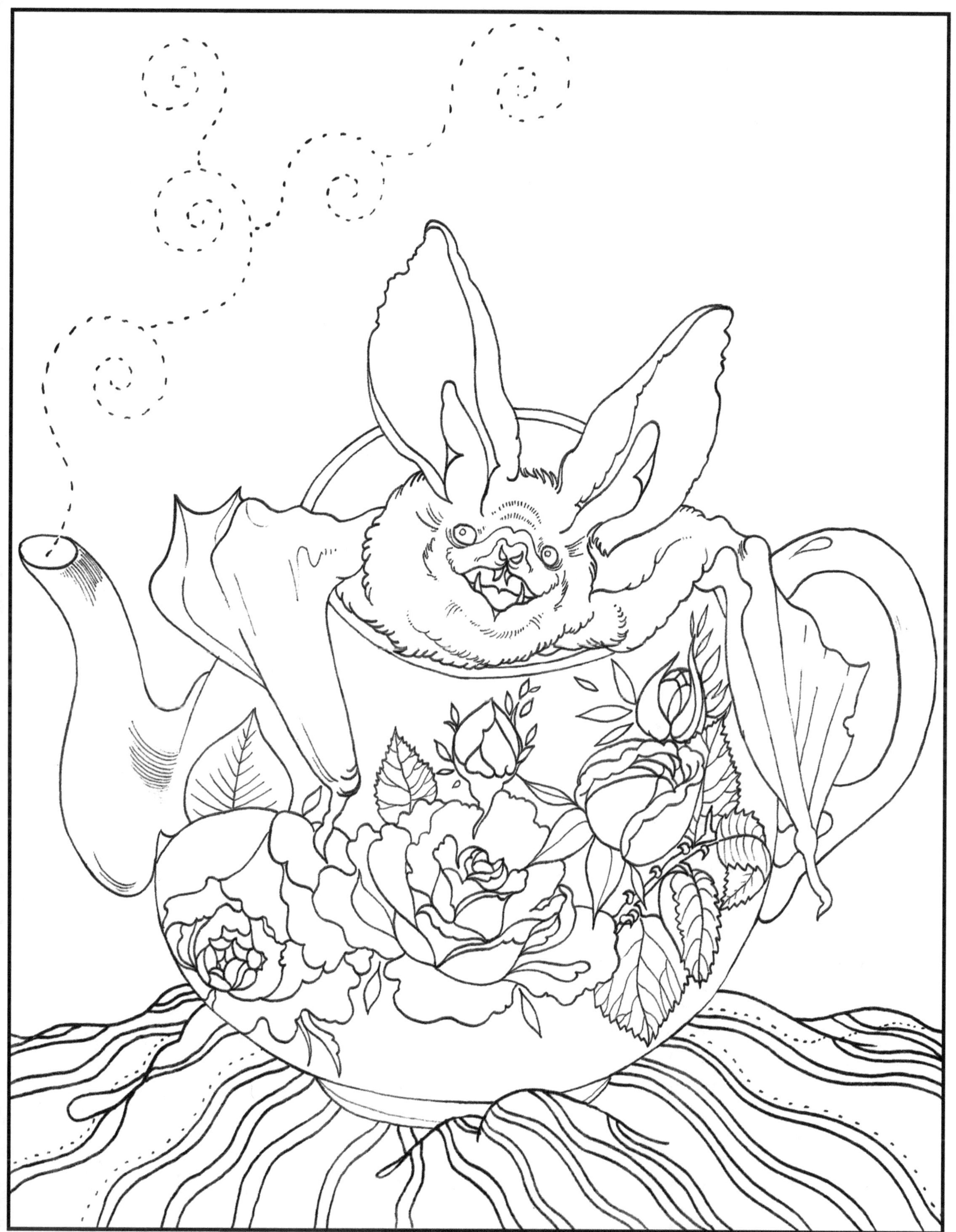

Adventures of the Old Teapot

Coloured By:

....

Date: ....

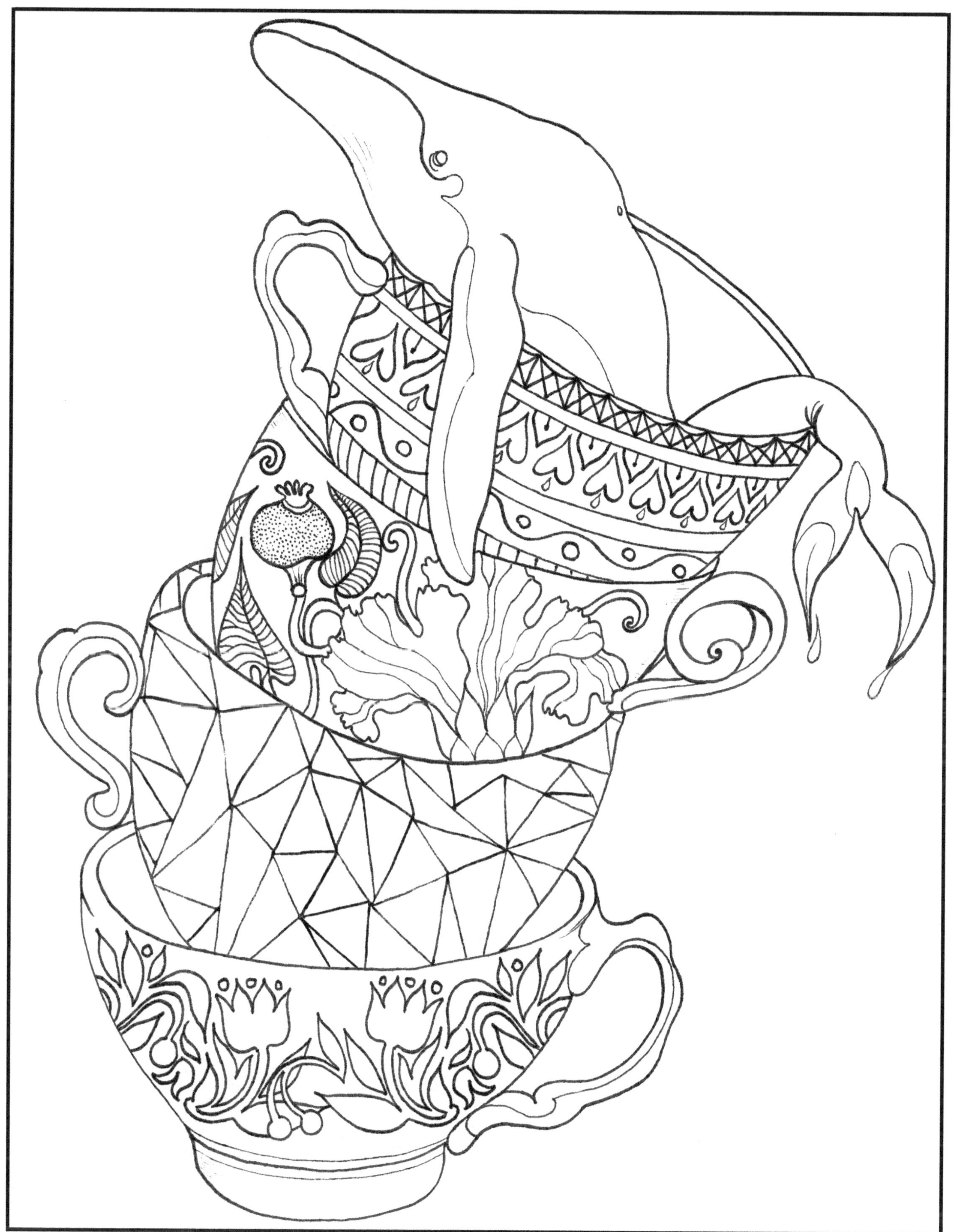

Nothing's Saner than Tea

Coloured By:

....

Date: ....

Coloured By:

....

Date: ....

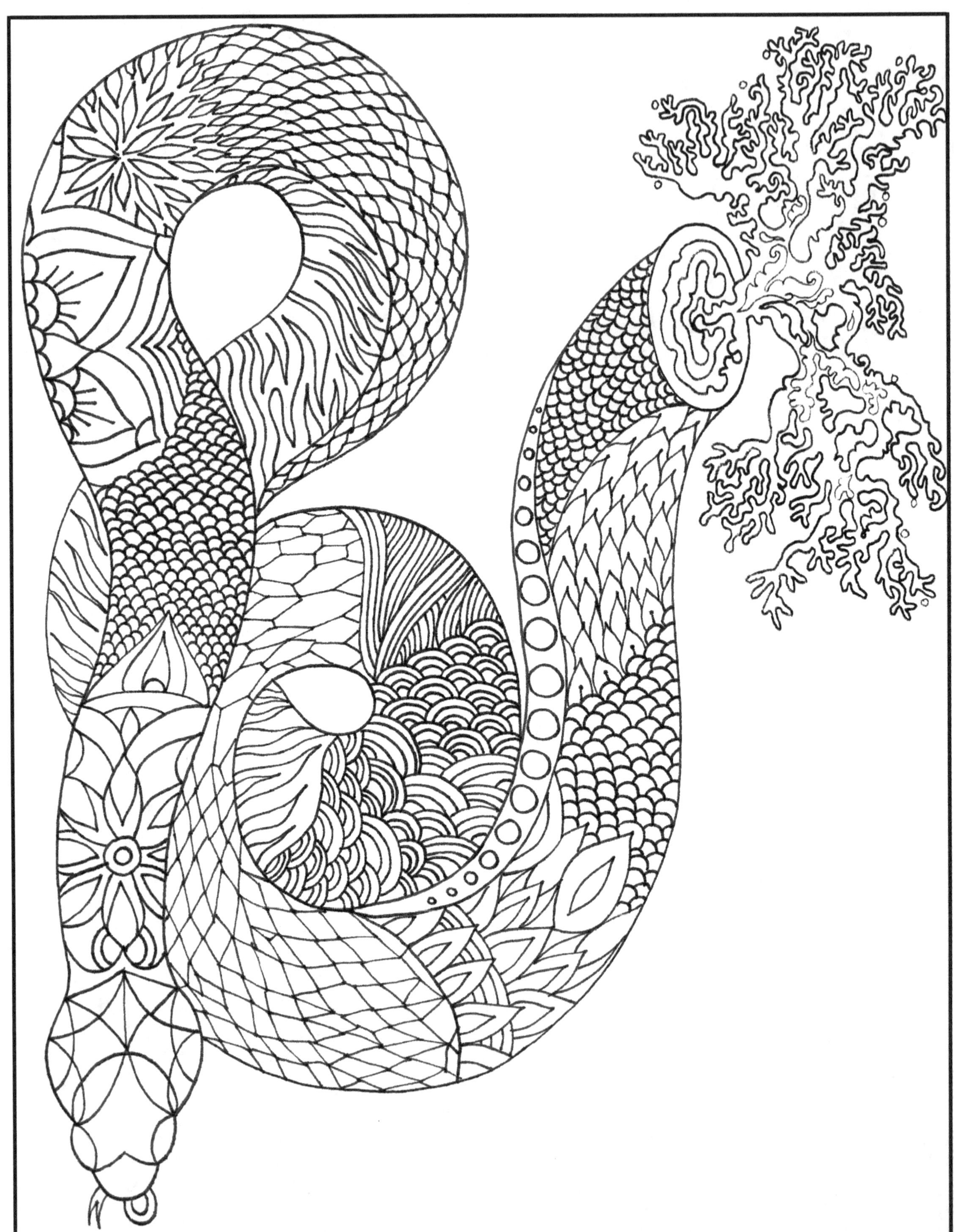

Among Sweet Flowers

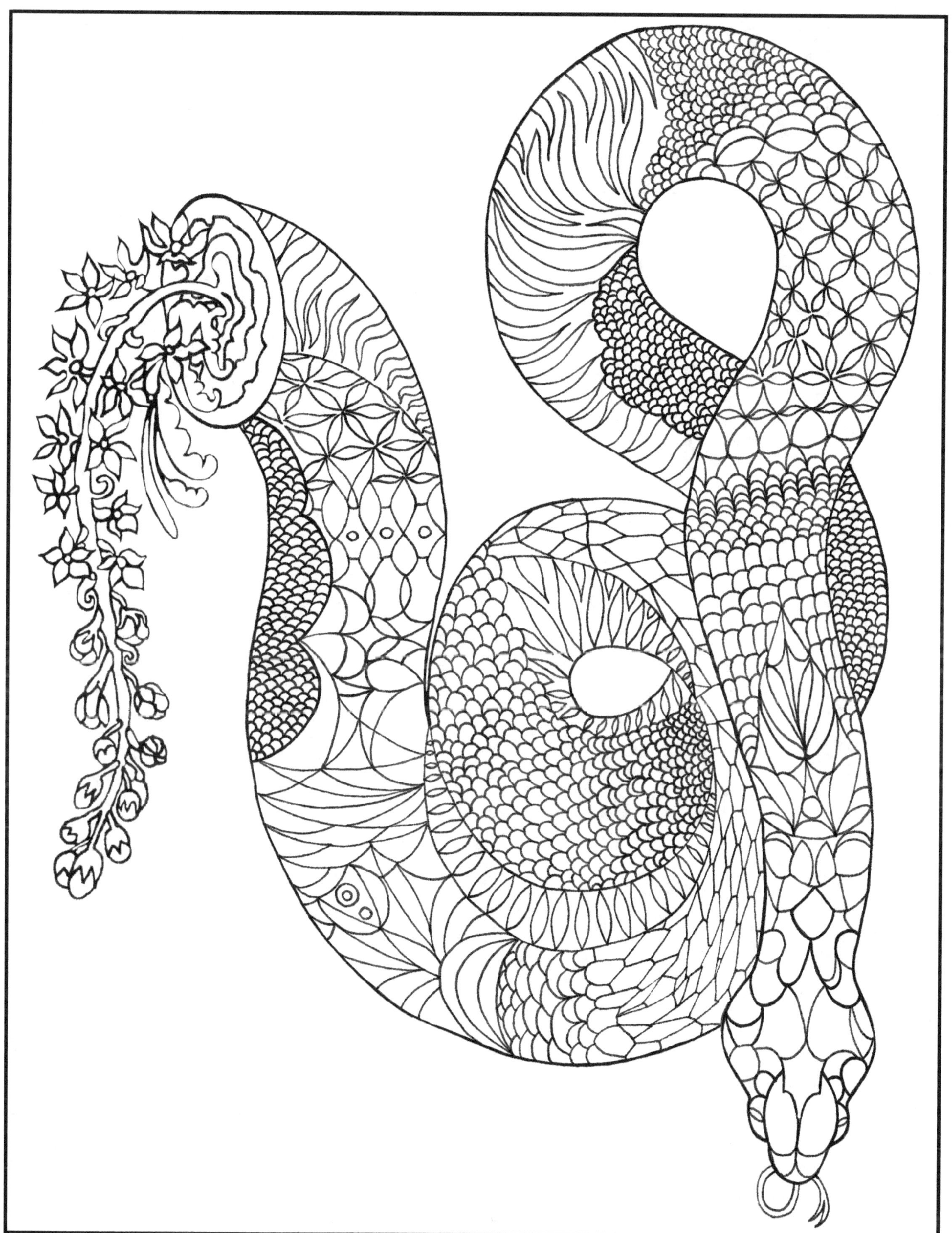

Among Sweet Flowers

Coloured By:

....

Date: ....

Coloured By:

....

Date: ....

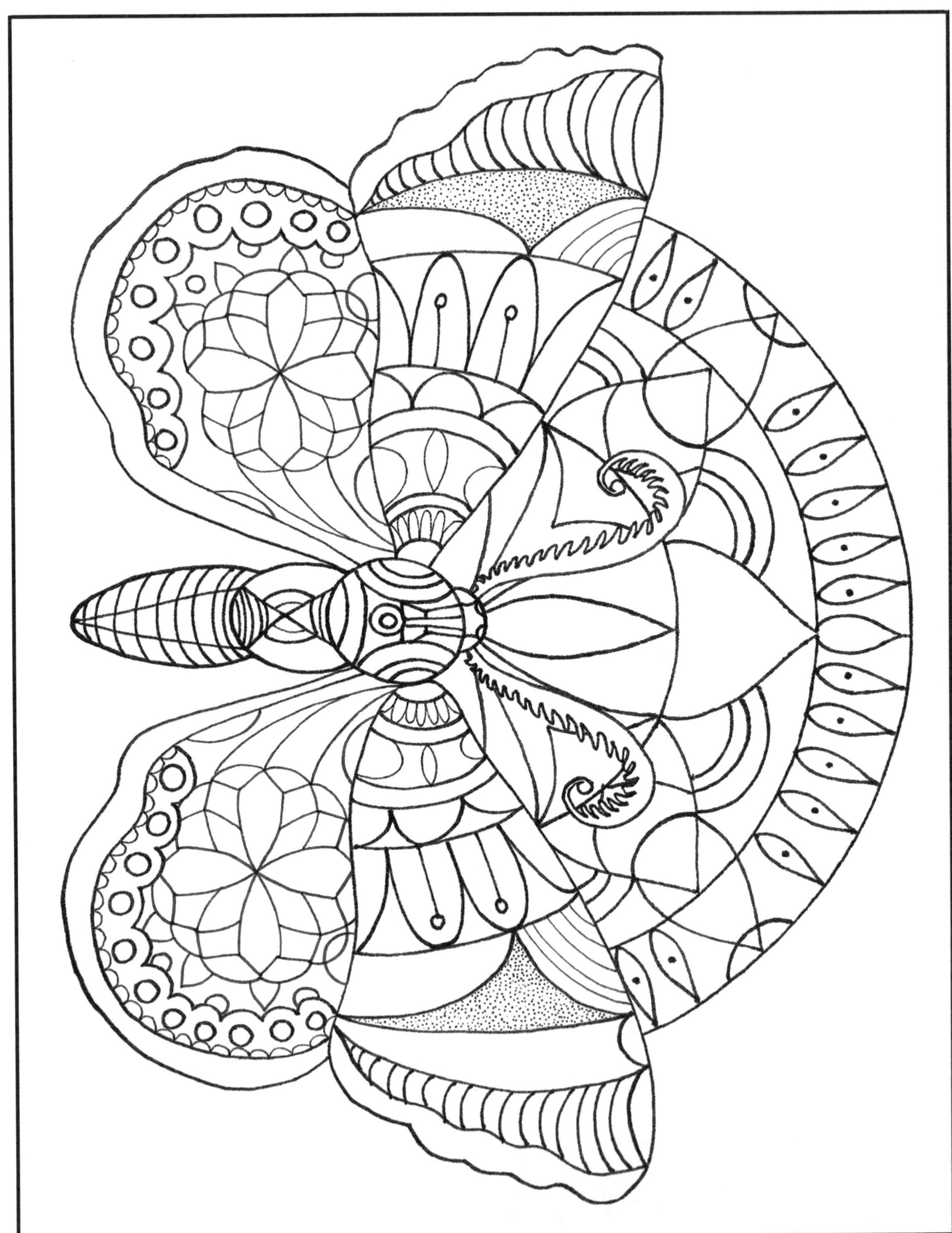

Moths and Light

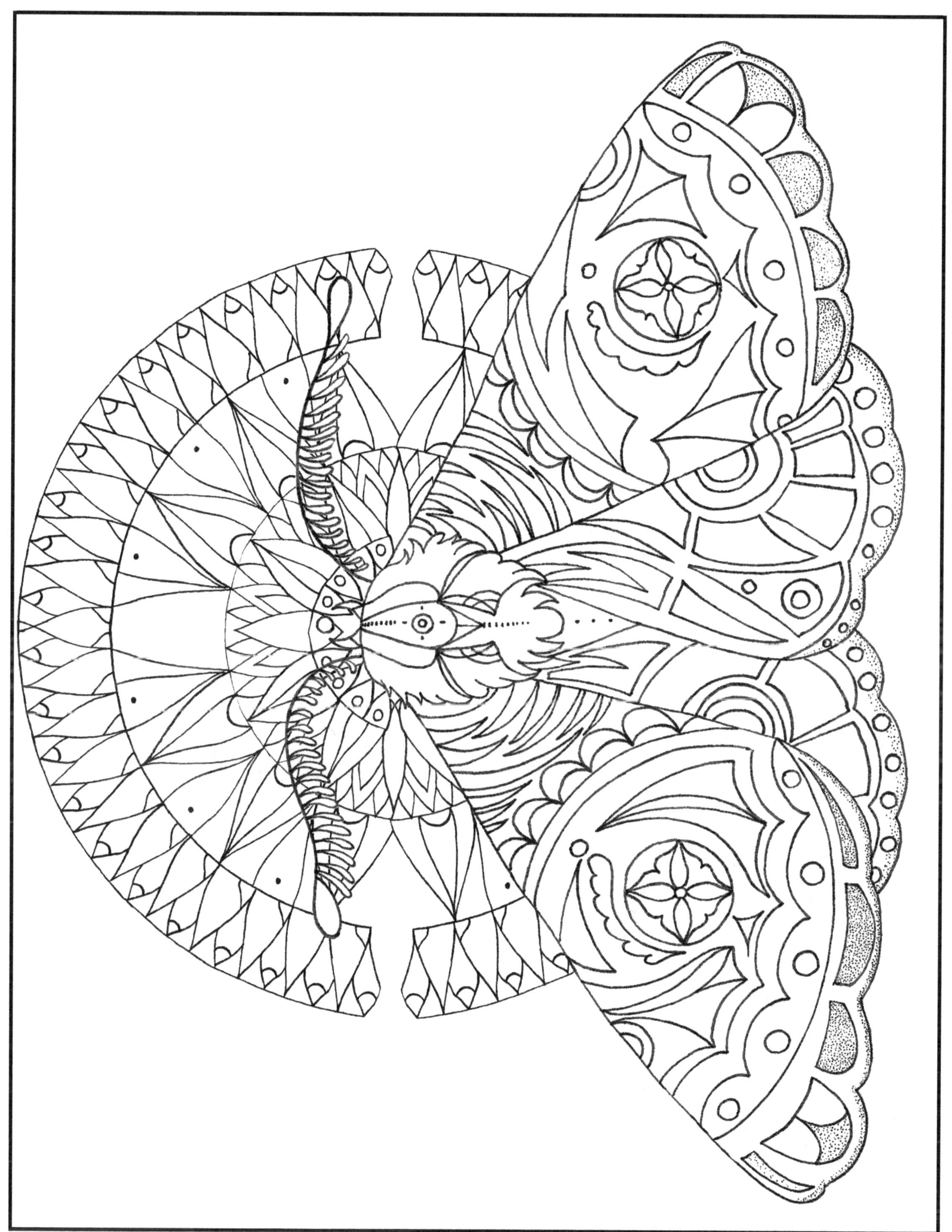

Moths and Light

Coloured By:

....

Date: ....

Coloured By:

....

Date: ....

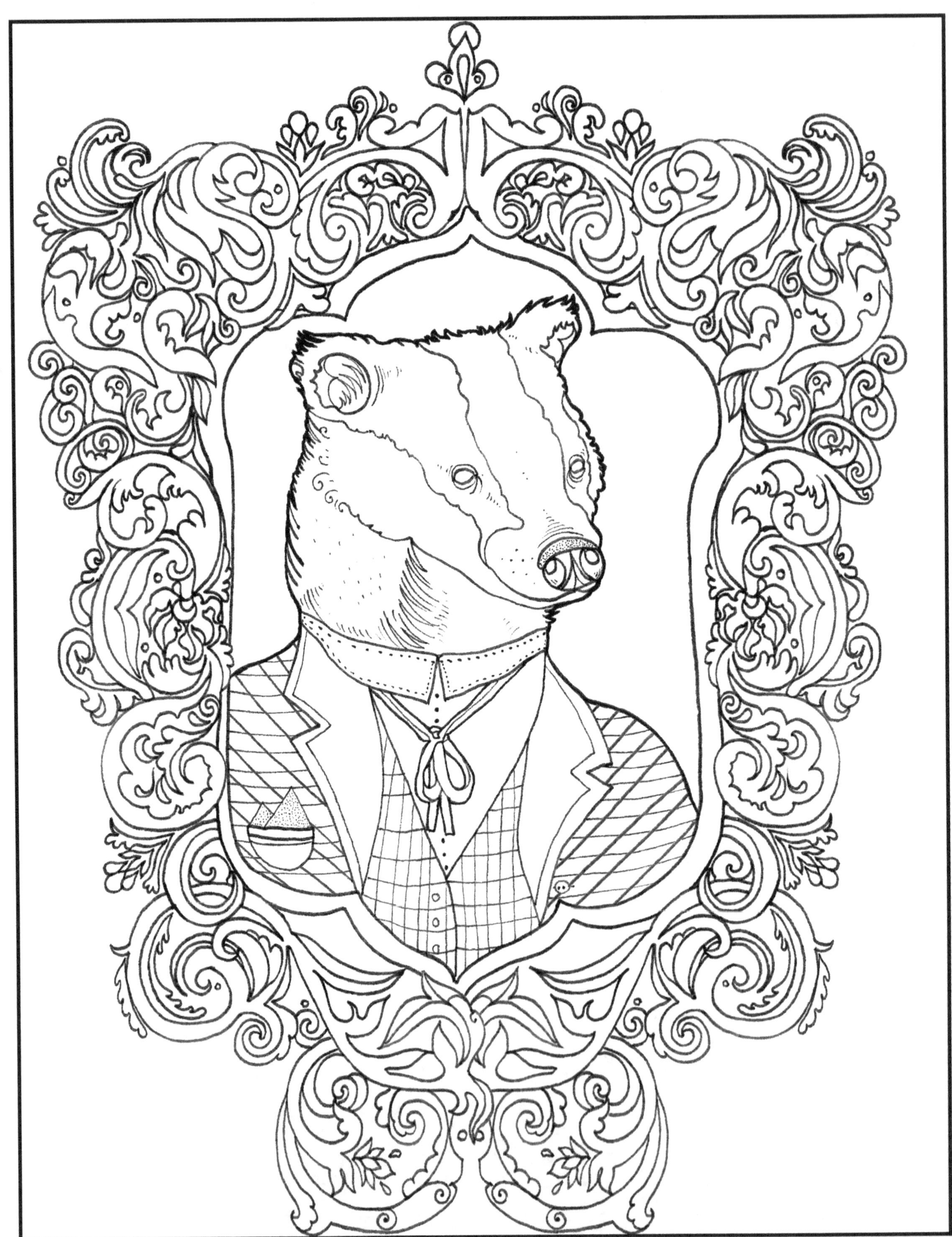

The Portrait of Mr Battersby

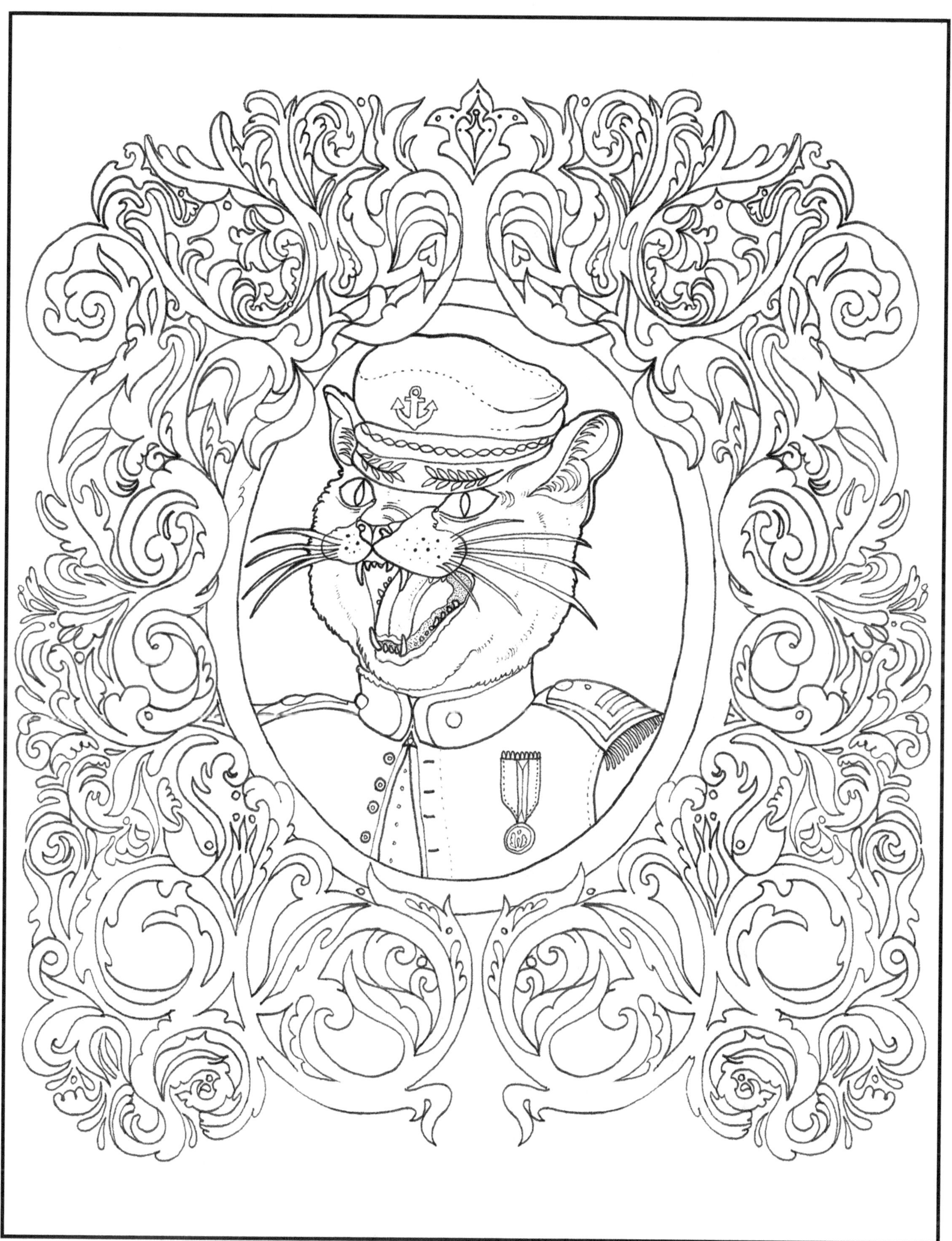

The Portrait of Captain Cantwell

Coloured By:

....

Date: ....

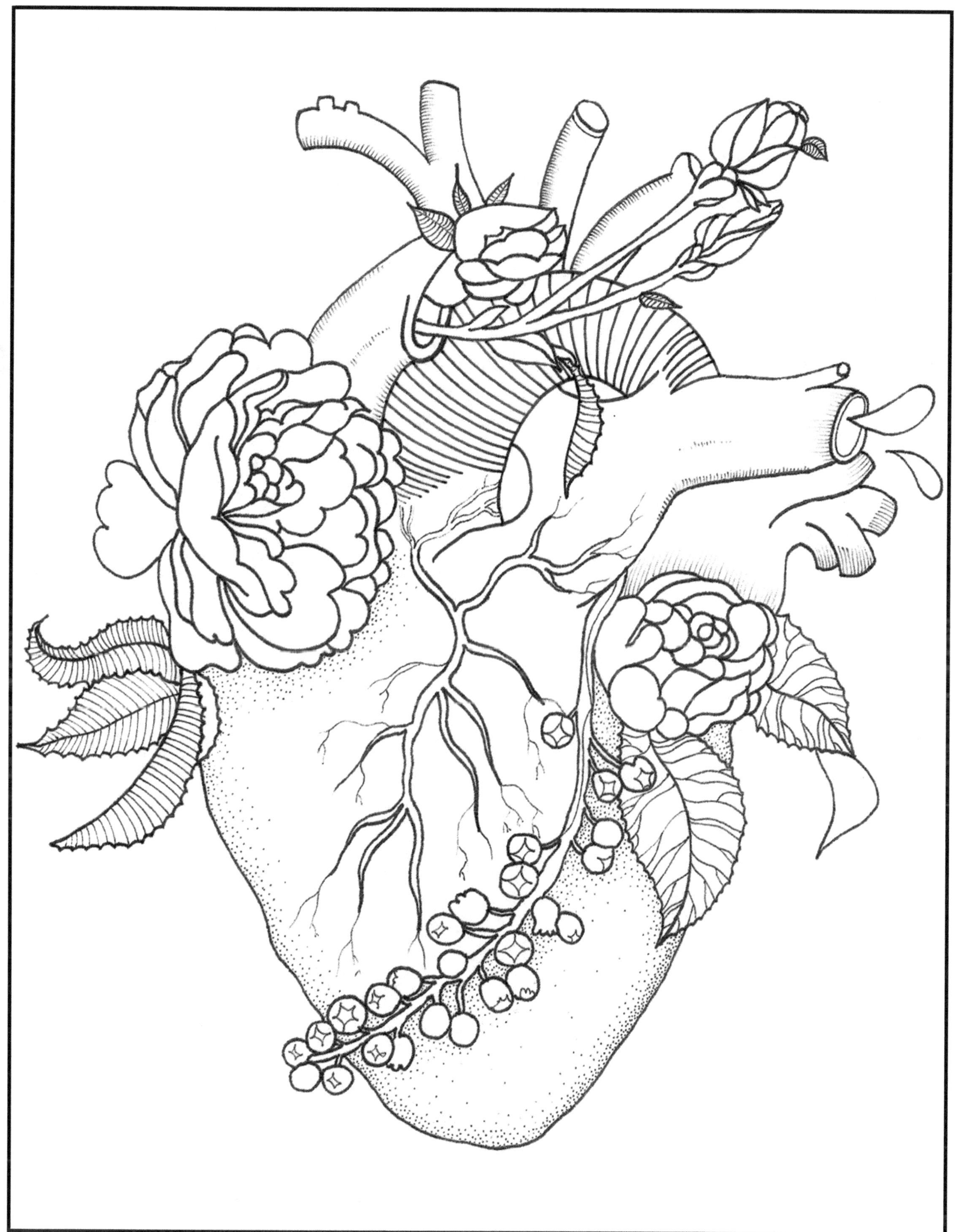

Pureheart

Coloured By:

....

Date: ....

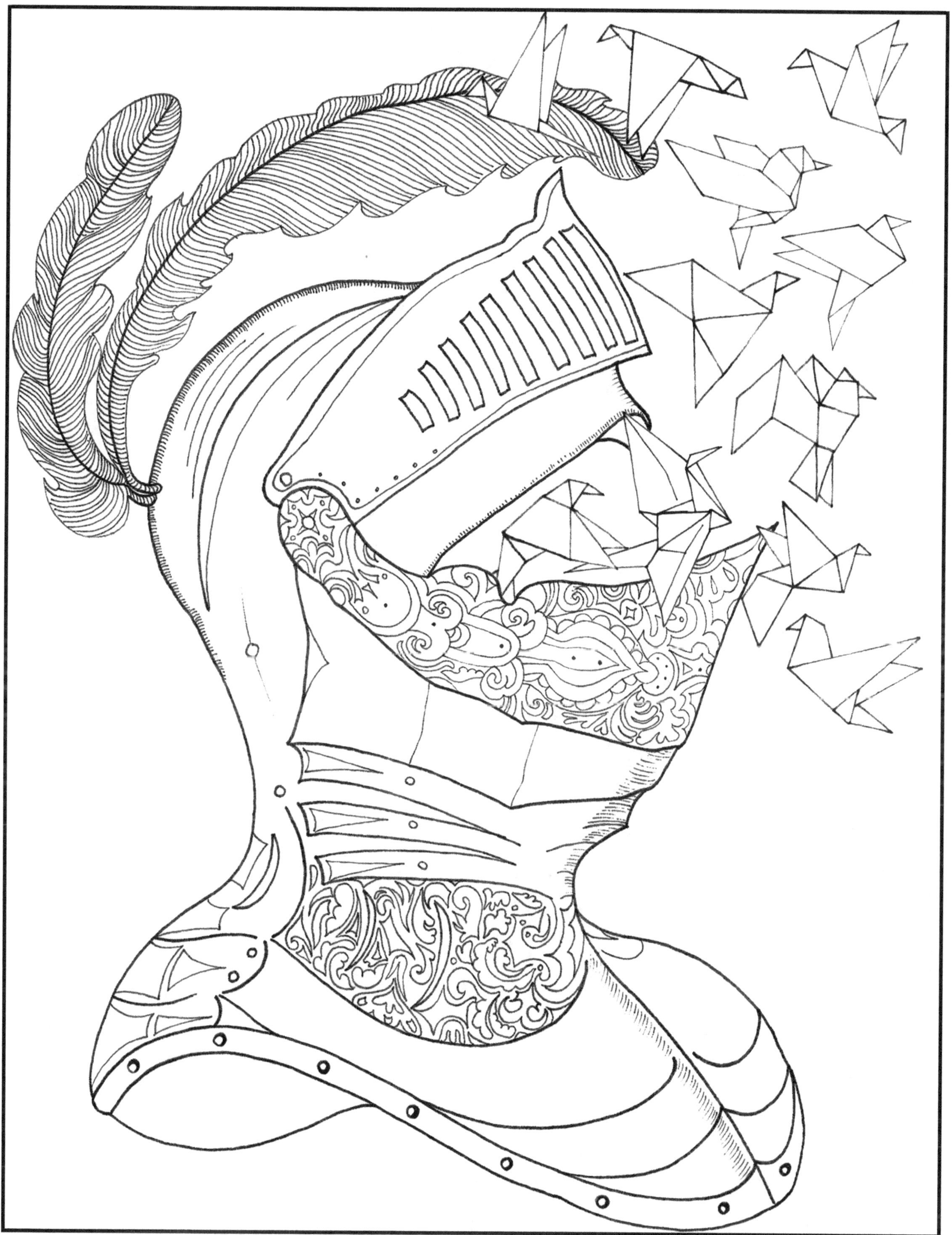

Have No Fear

Coloured By:

....

Date: ....

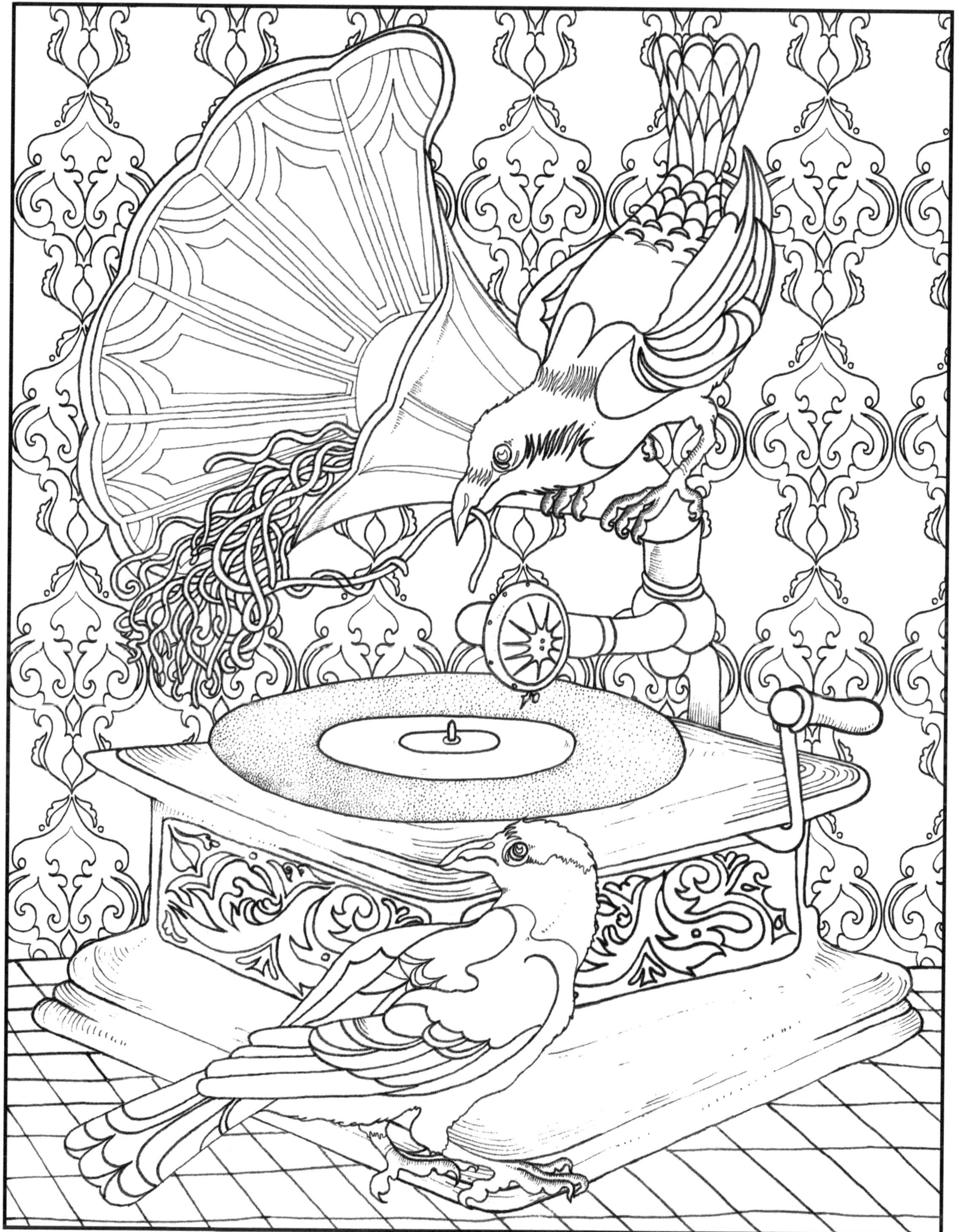

A Song to Die For

Coloured By:

....

Date: ....

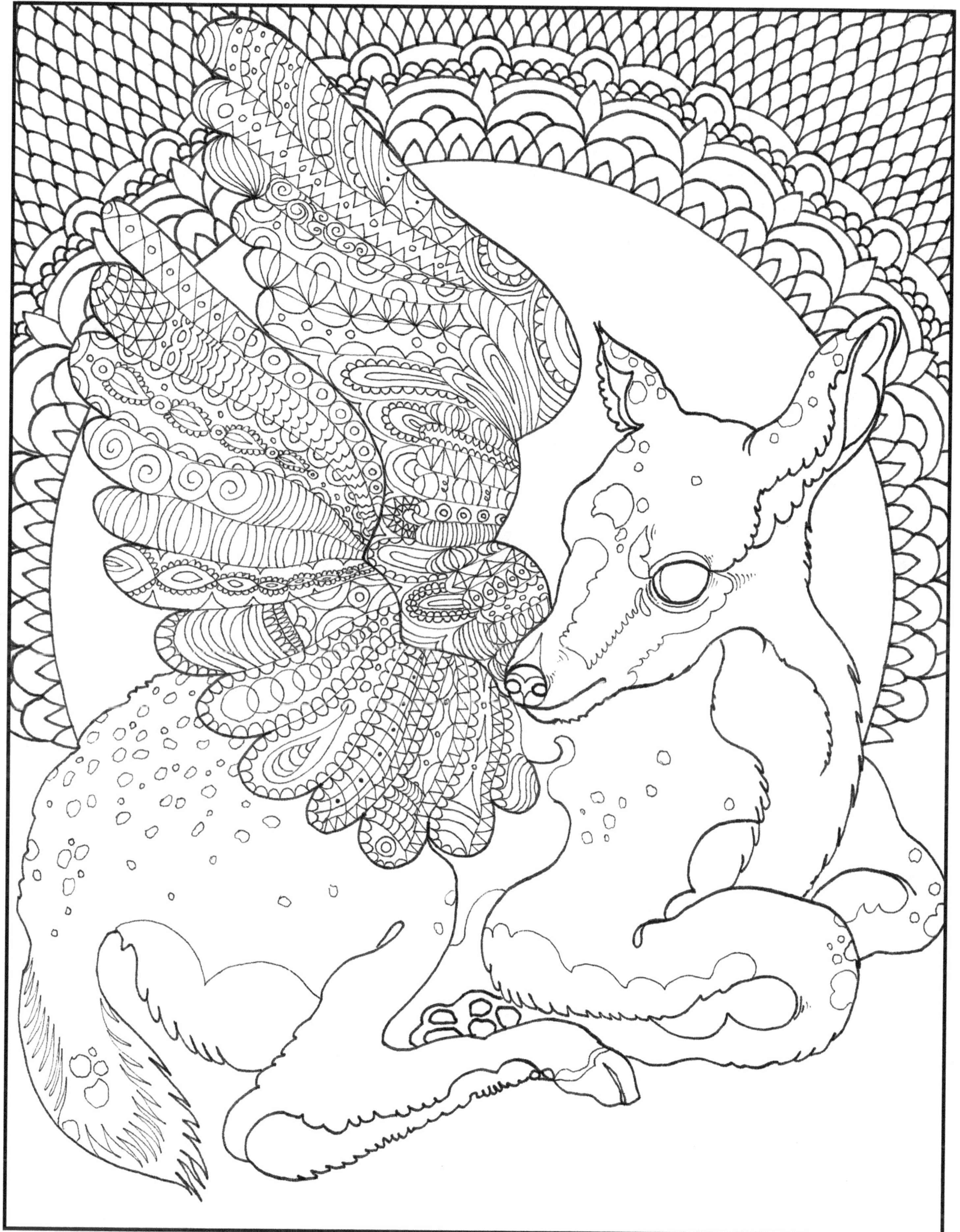

Fran's Hope

Coloured By:

....

Date: ....

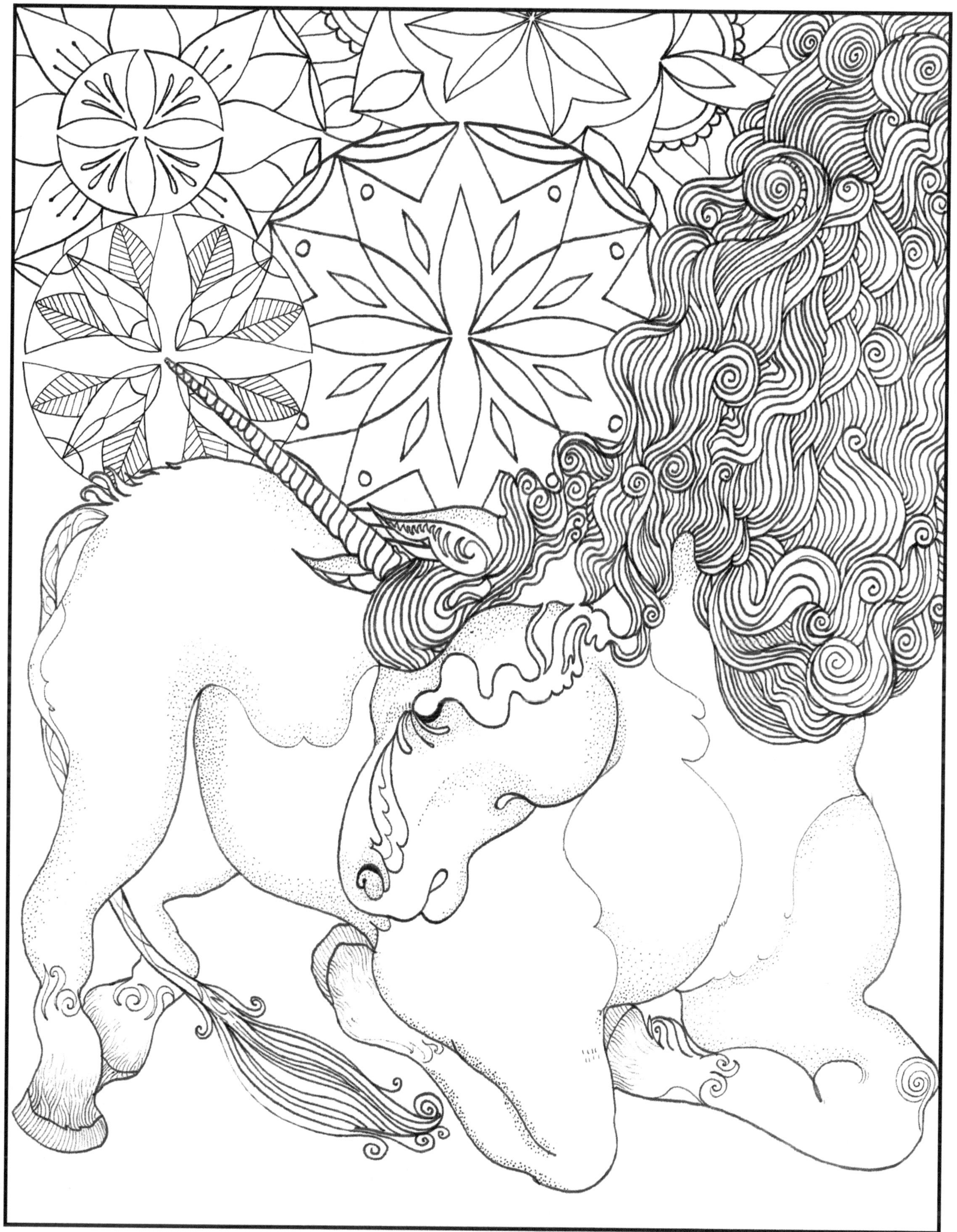

The Last Unicorn

Coloured By:

....

Date: ....

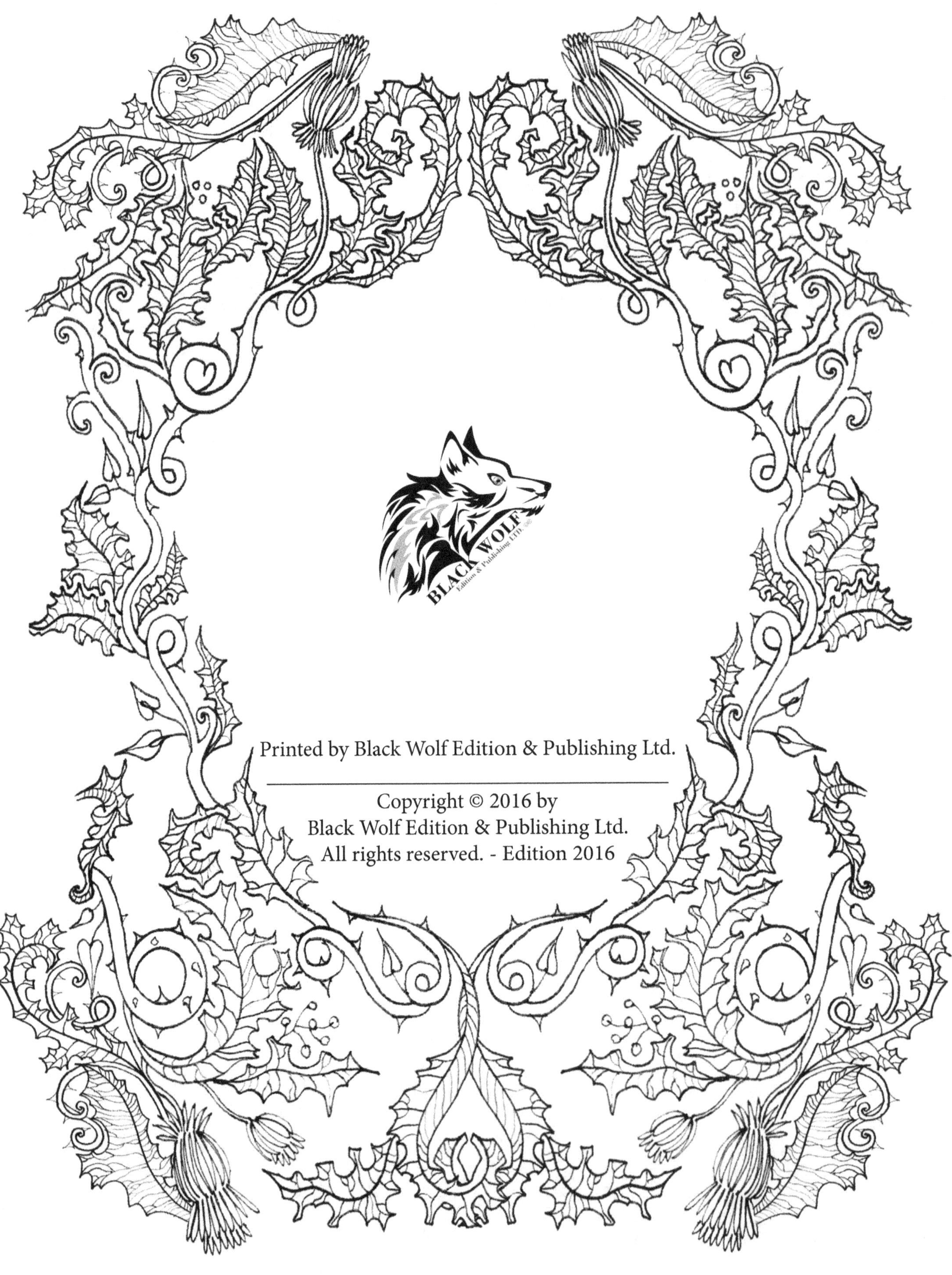
BLACK WOLF
Edition & Publishing LTD.

www.ingramcontent.com/pod-product-compliance
Lightning Source LLC
Chambersburg PA
CBHW080503030726
47592CB00011B/3231